DEDICATION:

To my father, Peter,
my spirit guide, and guardian angel.

Illustrations by
Lucy Pollard

HOW TO INTERPRET MESSAGES
FROM YOUR SPIRIT GUIDES

ANGEL NUMBERS

REMINGTON DONOVAN

Quadrille

CONTENTS

ANGEL NUMBERS

NUMEROLOGY IS A HIDDEN LANGUAGE OF THE UNIVERSE.

ONCE YOU UNLOCK IT, YOU WILL BEGIN TO SEE IT EVERYWHERE.

'I KEEP SEEING 333. WHAT DOES IT MEAN?'

INTRODUCTION

'Should I move to the address 754?'

'My son was born on 11/11.
Is he a special star crystal child?'

'I keep seeing 777, then 444 and 28.
What does it mean? I looked online, but I couldn't find a clear answer.'

The defining characteristic of numerology is that all numbers carry significance and can indeed convey a message. My emails, DMs and text messages are full of questions about the meaning of numbers, like the ones above. They have been filling my inbox for years. Finally, I decided to write a book in answer to 'What does it mean?', and here it is. It is a labour of love, my gift to you all (and to my inbox). Use it well.

HOW TO USE THIS BOOK

The interpretations in this book are rooted in the traditions of the Western Mystery tradition and Eastern Yogic philosophies and practices. In general, the Western schools are an amalgamation of Hermeticism, Rosicrucianism and Mystical Qabalah. Tarot, astrology and numerology are integral to this Western Mystery tradition.

Much of the numerology in this book is based on the Tree of Life, a symbol representing the interplay of the Universe. It consists of ten Sephiroth, which are considered the emanations of divinity. Each Sephiroth represents a different characteristic or archetype of the Universe and they are numbered one through to ten. My summary of these numbers reflects a lifetime of experience within these traditions. My goal for this book is to offer a guide that helps you have a more profound experience with numbers and, ultimately, a deeper experience of yourself. Use the meanings provided here as a springboard for your own consciousness. Trust your intuition. Numerology isn't meant to be a rigid spreadsheet. The idea is to allow the story to come to you. There isn't a wrong way to interpret it.

There is a spiritual teaching that states, 'Every number is infinite, and all are equal.' Therefore, don't view any number solely as a good sign or a bad sign. They are messages intended to help guide you for the better. A number that may seem negative can be a blessing, as it serves as a warning or a suggestion to alter your course. Conversely, a number that generally conveys a positive message might indicate that too much of a good thing is *not* a good thing.

I begin with triple numbers like 222, 777 or 444, which are generally called Angel numbers, and are regarded by many as a sign or a communication from something higher. All numbers carry significance and can indeed convey a message. Why do triples appear so relevant? The answer is rooted in the Qabalistic creation story of the Universe.

The first phase of creation was a single point in space. This is the number 1 and the first manifestation of God, known as *Kether*, the 'Crown'. This single point created itself out of itself, thereby creating two points in space. These two points form a line representing the concept of force, known as *Chokmah*, which means 'wisdom'. This is unhindered energy. Chokmah is considered the masculine archetype. In the Yogic traditions it is called the lingam. Next, a third point was created. These three points create a triangle, the first container. This idea of form is known as *Binah*, which means 'understanding'. It is this triangle that holds the energy. Binah is also considered the feminine archetype of the womb, called yoni in the Yogic traditions. The primary concept is that the number 3 is significantly stronger. It is the arena in which the metaphysical becomes physical.

Triple-digit numbers are significantly more discernible – they pop. This is because the energy of 3 conveys to our psyches that this is real and manifest. It has a stronger effect and carries more gravity. Imagine a container. This container holds the frequency and spiritual teachings associated with, in this case, the number.

When you start noticing a number, it is often the Universe, spirit guides, angels, God, Goddess or the great numerology oracle known as the microwave. Yes, I have seen the meme (which I love) of a satisfied-looking person who says, 'Seeing 11:11 on the microwave and knowing everything is going to be okay.' Whatever you choose to call a higher aspect of the Universe, it is giving you a message.

I also offer interpretations for the numbers 1 to 99 in this book. Knowing the meanings of these numbers will provide a powerful key to unlocking your own interpretations of any number.

For example, you might see 512 frequently and wonder what it signifies. Get creative and play around with it. You can decode this in several ways. Look up the meanings of 5, 1 and 2. The number 5 signifies action and removing obstacles, 1 represents connecting with your soul, and 2 symbolises forming strong connections with others. If this were my address, I would interpret it as maintaining a clean space that feels cosy when I'm alone and a wonderful place for friends, family and community. Alternatively, consider 51 and 2 or 5 and 12. The number 51 is about growth and learning, while 2 focuses on community and love. Perhaps you'll discover a new hobby or host more gatherings, making your home a true home. 5 is about taking action and 12 relates to desire and achieving your goals. This could be an excellent number for accomplishing your ambitions. There are many ways to approach this. You can also add all the digits of any number. For instance, 5 + 1 + 2 = 8. The number 8 represents life, healing and growth. It could also represent a calendar date, like May 12th if you read dates the American way, or 5th December in the UK. This may prove significant. Through this small example, you can see how easily it flows together.

This is about your message and your story. As I mentioned, there are no strict rules. Feel free to integrate this book's interpretations with your own traditions, beliefs and insights. Numerology is universal. It is less about the specific meaning of a number and more about broadening your perspective to approach a situation with greater wisdom. Follow where it leads you, and don't forget to have fun.

NUMEROLOGY

WHAT IS NUMEROLOGY AND HOW TO PRACTISE IT

Numerology isn't a study as much as a practice. A practice that, over time, will increase your intuition and, therefore, your awareness. Not just with numbers but also with the world around you.

Numerology is a hidden language of the Universe. Once you unlock it, you will begin to see it everywhere. A balanced approach is important. I have met people who keep notebook upon notebook, logging number after number, searching for answers that never appear. And I have seen people share an alignment of number after number, oblivious to its significance. You can't force insights. Start paying attention and with a relaxed mind, an artistic approach and a little practice, you will become adept at discerning if a number is a message – or merely a number. It is wise to know that sometimes a number is just a number! I recently had a good friend message me, asking if they should book a flight that left at 3:33. I told them I wouldn't make travel arrangements based on the numerology of departure times. Book the flight if you want to get to where you're going. You'll drive yourself crazy trying to game the best numbers.

OBSERVE REPETITION. OFTEN, A SPECIFIC NUMBER WILL KEEP APPEARING TO YOU.

You may find yourself checking the clock at the same time every day, only to spot that same number on an address or a deli ticket. What matters isn't the source, but the consistency.

For example, one day, I kept seeing the number 17. My groceries came to £71.17. I parked behind a car with 1717 on its number plate. I went to a café; not only was my total £17.17, but my order number was 17. I messaged my now-wife, who was in Venice, Italy, to tell her that even I, a professional numerologist, couldn't believe how often I was seeing 17. She decided to go to a casino and bet on 17 at the roulette table. We're not into gambling at all, but she won 170 Euros. At the time, we had just begun dating. When she returned, we went on our first weekend away, and our hotel room number was 17. From then on, we considered 17 to be one of our numbers. In my practice, one of the associations of 17 is the Star card in Tarot, which is attributed to the astrological sign Aquarius. Both our children are Aquarians. For the mythology of my family, 17 is significant. For me, 17 is always a reminder of them. Pay attention: you will find your own numbers, which will become significant and have their own mythology.

The practice of numerology is not memorisation, analysis and calculation; this is a small part of the process. Numerology is storytelling; it is art and poetry. The meanings shared in this book are intended to be a gateway to a higher consciousness, a consciousness within you. Numerology serves as a springboard to help you tell your story.

This practice is about you and your growth. Numerology is mysticism. Mystics are considered unifiers. The mystic understands the interconnectedness of all things. In numerology, there are no coincidences. Numerology is a practice that taps into the mystery of you. There is a teaching in this tradition that I love. 'The history is His story; the mystery is My story.' With practice, you will decipher meanings no one else could, because this is about you and your story.

NUMBERS ARE A SIGN AND A CLUE TO A BIGGER PICTURE. THEY ARE LIKE PUZZLE PIECES CONNECTING A BIGGER STORY. THEY CONNECT DOTS YOU DIDN'T THINK TO CONNECT BEFOREHAND.

Take the meanings I lay out in this book and then get creative. It is the practice of numerology, acting as a meditation, that will open you up, not rigid definitions of numbers. This meditative approach trains you to have greater awareness and understanding. Ultimately, it is a more profound experience with your infinite self. Through that, greater truth will be revealed. More importantly, you will begin to understand what it means for you – your story.

Numerology is not fortune-telling. Knowing what will happen is fate, while knowing what to do is destiny. Numbers are divine messengers. They do predict but overall, they serve as a call to action, indicating what needs to be done for further success. The question isn't 'What will happen to me?' Instead, it is 'What must I do?'

ANGEL NUMBERS

111

You are in the right place, and now is the right time. Positive changes are happening fast, and you are blessed with new opportunities. This is the start of something favourable. 111 is a clean slate. Pursue this new endeavour with zeal. 111 is the creative potential of the Universe. Harness and direct it. You have the full force of the Creator behind you. You can create what you want. The Universe is asking you to make the first move. Infinite potential is with you. Anything is possible.

111 is regarded as the primordial point at which the entire Universe was created. You are brimming with potential now; it is your job to bring that potential to life. What do you desire? You are being called to manifest it. 111 is reminding you that you can conjure it from thin air. You possess the Universe's creative force

at your fingertips. Begin where you are. Momentum is on your side. There is an all-knowing aspect to 111 that transcends intellect, and there will be ample time to figure it out as you proceed.

1 is the number of the soul. Your soul represents you – the true you – and your divine purpose. When you create from your soul, it comes from an authentic place. In Qabalah, the first Sephirah is known as *Kether*, meaning 'crown'. It is attributed to Pluto and the colour white. Pluto embodies the truth and purity of your soul. Your soul knows everything and what you truly desire in this life. Pluto facilitates powerful transformations. It is an emancipator, allowing you to become your authentic self while embracing your unadulterated truth.

111 represents the spiritual crown and a precious jewel. It symbolises your most divine self. 111 is a message to harmonise with this truth, serving as a source of all wisdom, knowledge and creation. Additionally, it encourages you to remain true and honourable to that source. This is you co-creating with the Creator. You are now in the zone.

OVERALL, 111 IS AN INSPIRING AND PROMISING NUMBER. IT IS A SIGN OF GOOD TIMES AHEAD, A HOPEFUL NEW BEGINNING.

It's like the feeling of the first day at university or the first day at a new dream job: you got in or you got hired, and the journey starts now.

Several years ago, I had the chance to write a story for a successful film franchise. My story made it to the top of the list at the studio, competing with a few other pitches from different writers. I was anxious to find out if it would get the green light. For me, as a Hollywood no-name, it would be a life-changing moment and the start of a new journey. In the days leading up to the verdict, I began to see 111. Not a lot, but enough to catch my attention. My story featured a cartoon with ninjas and a chicken. Suddenly, I saw 111 again, along with a guy wearing a T-shirt with ninjas on it. I felt this was Spirit confirming the green light. And it was.

111 is ecstatic. It conveys a message of lightness and freedom – the freedom to pursue what you've always desired but felt too ashamed or afraid to embrace. You are encouraged to dance as if no one is watching. The childlike innocence of 111 liberates you from self-imposed restrictions such as doubt, shame and guilt. It's truly freeing. 111 lightens the load. The weight of the world is lifting off your shoulders.

There is no notion of failure here; everything is a success, even when you think it's not. Approach the world as if everything is your favourite thing. This is the essence of 111. With this mindset, everything becomes a success, even if you have to 'fake it until you make it'.

111 is optimistic, evoking a wide-eyed enthusiasm. It suggests an attitude shift: embrace a sense of innocent wonder. Yogic teaching says to treat all experiences as a delightful piece of fruit, and 111 is this delightful fruit.

TRUST YOUR INTUITION

BE MINDFUL

111 is so free and fun that you should be cautious about being overly foolish. Don't let optimism and zeal be the fuel for ridiculous decisions. Maintain a childlike innocence, while exercising discernment. On the flip side, this could result in you becoming stagnant and uninspired. Keep it fresh, and keep it moving.

PROSPERITY PRACTICE

111 is an inspired new journey – a fresh start. Do something different daily. Often, this is done for 40 days. For instance, if you always take the same route to work, try a new one. Sample a different food or restaurant, or begin a new hobby. If you usually put your left shoe on first, start with your right. The choice is yours. Keep it new and lively, and see where it takes you. It's meant to be fun.

111

IS:

MAKING THE FIRST MOVE

BRIMMING WITH POTENTIAL

NEW BEGINNINGS

CREATIVE FORCE

FUN TIMES AHEAD

222

You are on the right track. You have the momentum; smooth sailing is ahead. Spirit is saying yes; you should, too. This is the sweet spot. Your longing will be satisfied. 222 is blessing you with a life of contentment and joy. Opportunities abound. Allow yourself to receive and connect with them. Be easy-going and open-minded about it. Flow with your intuition. More is being revealed; you never know what might appear. The lucky stars are favouring you.

This number confirms that you should stay on your path. You've embarked on this journey, and this is the honeymoon phase of your endeavour, meant to inspire and energise you. This is the easy part, so enjoy it. Keep your eye on the prize. If you keep up, you will be kept up. 222 also signifies safe travels.

222 is a message to be open and honest. Wear your heart on your sleeve. Show your true colours: 222 reminds you that you are a brilliant rainbow. Honesty is the best approach. Be genuine. The only thing you can be is yourself. There's a teaching I love: 'The Universe is ready to serve you, if you just be you.' It's so simple, yet many of us find it challenging. We hide who we are and fail to express ourselves. 222 is your reminder to embrace your true self. Say yes to yourself. Stop living a lie. The truth of who you are will set you free. From this place, trust that you will attract the destiny you are meant to fulfil.

**THE STARS ARE ALIGNING.
IT'S ALL COMING TOGETHER NOW.
THE ANSWER IS YES.
WHAT IS THE QUESTION?**

222 is known as the illuminating intelligence. More will be revealed. If you feel stuck or in the dark about something, know a light will shine on it. Also, be the

light. Brighten up someone else's day. Be a force of good in the world. Stay on the sunny side of life.

2 on its own represents open-mindedness. It longs to belong, unify and receive. In Mystical Qabalah, the second Sephirah is known as *Chokmah*, meaning 'wisdom'. Both Neptune and Uranus are associated with this number as well as the colour grey. It's fitting that two planets embody the essence of the number 2. Neptune teaches us how to merge with the greater Universe, while Uranus promotes positive change and hopeful possibilities. The number 222 expands on this idea, encouraging us to merge with a greater purpose and broader possibilities.

This is a message of vulnerability and tenderness. Allow yourself to be open to your higher intuition. 222 is like love at first sight. When you know, you know. This is your true understanding. With vulnerability, you will attract everything you need and opportunities you never thought possible. Fall in love with your life, and you will have a life you love. From there, everything else will unfold. This is 222.

If you're single, 222 is a powerful sign that you may meet a partner. Keep an open mind; 222 loves love. Love yourself, and others will as well. If you are in a relationship, fall even more in love.

New connections are now being made, and old connections are strengthening their bonds. This is a fortunate message for family, friends and your community. Socialise, host a soirée, go out on the town or go on a date.

I once visited Toronto, Canada, because my wife had been working on a film there all winter. Before I left sunny Los Angeles for freezing Toronto, I started spotting 222, a number I love to see. I was very optimistic about my visit. On the other hand, my wife had been there for months, enduring the cold, and she was over it. But I kept seeing 222 everywhere. I even joked that 222 was the official number of Toronto. I wasn't going to let the cold get me down. Granted, I wasn't working 18-plus hour days and was a tourist.

Before I arrived, my wife attended a yoga studio, and when they found out I was her partner, they couldn't believe it. That already made me feel appreciated. They invited me to teach a numerology workshop, and I said yes. Remember, 222 is big yes energy. I assumed only a few people would attend. Much to my surprise, it turned out to be a standing-room-only event. I met so many wonderful people and built a loving community. I loved Canada, even in the cold.

BE MINDFUL

222 represents longing, which can lead to the fear of missing out, commonly known as FOMO. This number embodies a yearning for gratification. The lesson is to foster a sense of contentment while connecting to your divine self. When you stop wanting, everything you want will begin to want you. Given that 222 is a significant number associated with connections, be mindful of isolation and detachment. It is the message of yes. Are you saying no too often, or shutting yourself off from new opportunities? On the other hand, be wary of naivety and being too trusting. You can achieve great things by maintaining a positive attitude and practising moderation.

PROSPERITY PRACTICE

222 is the number of loving connections and appreciation. 222 loves life. A great practice if you are seeing 222 is an attitude of gratitude. Write down at least three things for which you are grateful each day. This has the most impact when done first thing in the morning. It sets a good tone for the day. However you decide to do it, know that 222 is a message to stay grateful.

222

IS:

YOU ARE ON A ROLL NOW

HONEYMOON PHASE

LOVE AT FIRST SIGHT

YES IS A COMPLETE SENTENCE

LONGING TO BELONG

WHEN YOU KNOW, YOU KNOW

333

333 separates the pros from the amateurs. You are being blessed with managerial ability and big boss energy, so conduct yourself with dignity. 333 is a manifestation. This is a message that you are getting close, but there is still work to be done. Do what is needed to actualise your dreams. The Universe wants you to succeed. 333 is doing your part. As the saying goes, God helps those who help themselves.

The good news is that 333 usually shows up because you are on the verge of tremendous success. But in order to have the success you want, you need to go back over your work. It is a message to check all the details. Get into the nitty-gritty. This is because 333 is an unresolved issue. It is a warning that something is coming back to haunt you. Resolve it. Perhaps you have a big presentation for a new client.

Go back over everything. Are you missing anything? Make sure you are prepared. If you see 333 before a trip, check your packing. Do you have your passport? Are the reservations in order? Don't leave room for error. Maybe you are turning in an article or manuscript for publication. If you keep seeing 333, go back over it. For example, I have been seeing 333 consistently ever since I started writing this book.

3 is the number of building, work and gumption. It is making something real, tangible and manifest. It is also known as the positive mind: sharp, analytical and dignified. 3 has a remarkable ability to understand the situation and what needs to be done. In Qabalah, the third Sephirah is known as *Binah*, meaning 'understanding'. Saturn and the colour black are attributed here. Saturn is the taskmaster. She is disciplined and focused. Saturn gets what Saturn wants because she works for it. 3 and Saturn teach us that no job is too big or small to be accomplished. 333 is a more potent version of that. This is a message to do the work to actualise your dreams.

It is time to face the music. Something from your past is showing up again; this could be both a good and a bad thing. Usually, it is something you thought you had resolved, but it shows up again because it needs addressing. It is finally time to roll back that rug you swept everything under. It is also about addressing all the things you keep putting off. What have you been avoiding?

333 is a message that everything is escalating; it's getting real. You are so close, so don't sabotage your success by succumbing to inertia. The Universe is asking you to get a grip on the situation, roll up your sleeves and be a pro. Use 333's powers of analysis. What is being overlooked? Check every detail. Don't make it a big deal that you have extra work. Be grateful the Universe is making you aware of issues that must be addressed.

On a personal level, it can be a message to examine behaviours you thought you had overcome and that are showing up again. For example, maybe you stopped drinking or smoking, but you're becoming increasingly tempted to start again. The message is clear: don't do it.

I frequently see 333 when I'm buying junk food. My spirit guide says, 'Dude, this isn't going to be good for you and will come back to haunt you in the form of metabolic dysfunction.' Clearly, my alter ego spirit guide speaks like a surfer guy. I often see 333 when I am visiting New York City. I was born there, and my family goes back five generations. I can't help but think it is a message about my unresolved family issues.

I once had a client message me that all day she saw 555 (often a number of conflicts) and 333. I joked about getting ready for a fight because something was about to pop up for her. Later that day, she messaged me that she had strep throat and was fighting it with antibiotics. This was a perfect alignment. Of course, this doesn't mean you will get sick if you see 333. It is a message that something needs to be addressed.

333 is also a powerful sign that what you are working on is about to be manifested. It is considered the number of a container – a container that receives. The spiritual teaching is to make yourself a fit receptacle. It encourages us to examine what we

want to create and manifest. What needs to happen to get us there? Let's say you want to manifest a significant amount of money. What vessel can receive this money? What are you creating that might generate income? Is it a lemonade stand? Or an advanced professional training that will increase your ability to get a promotion? Maybe you aspire to become a doctor. To do so, you must put in the work of attending medical school and everything else involved. I call this the 'life on life's terms' adulting number. What must you do to have your goals come to fruition? A traditional attribution means to 'bring into capture'. If we abstract this a bit, it refers to what is under your control or what needs to be tightened up. The message is to do more to attain and capture, if you will, your goals.

333 IS A POWERFUL SIGN THAT WHAT YOU ARE WORKING ON IS ABOUT TO BE MANIFESTED.

BE MINDFUL

333 is a message to be the boss and taskmaster and to get the job done. It is the labour before harvesting the fruit. Hard work is a virtue, but be conscious of where you are toiling without reward. This is similar to the famous proverb, 'All work and no play makes Jack a dull boy.' It could be a message you're too uptight. Loosen your tie or slip into something more comfortable and make time for leisure.

PROSPERITY PRACTICE

Since 333 is often a message of unresolved issues, here is a great practice to start resolving. I call it the loose-ends practice. Make a list of all the loose ends in your life. Big and small. From that lightbulb in the cupboard that needs changing to the website you need to build for your new business. What is keeping you up at night? Make the list and start crossing it off one by one. You will be surprised how much you will begin to get done. Try and do one thing a day.

333

IS:

A BOSS

WORK ETHIC

ADULTING

TIME TO FACE THE MUSIC

UNRESOLVED ISSUES

444

The Universe is showering you so many with blessings, supporting and loving you. Good things are coming your way. Opportunity is knocking; open the door. Have faith that Spirit always provides. Bliss, ease and peace are in the works. This is your gentle reminder that it is all going to work out. This is for the higher good.

This is the number of miracles. Something better than you imagine is in store for you. Keep it simple, don't overthink it, get out of the way and allow it. Allowing is a key practice of 444.

444 is the number of perfect love. Higher love. Universal love. Revel in it. Remember, all you need is love.

444 IS A RELIEF FROM HARDSHIP, CONFLICTS, AND BURDENS.

4 is the number of mercy, compassion and love. It is called the neutral mind, giving it objectivity and a natural sense of fairness. In Qabalah, the fourth Sephirah is *Chesed*, meaning 'mercy'. Jupiter is attributed to Chesed as well as the colour blue. Jupiter teaches generosity, abundance and blessings. It's a high roller who wants to pay for everyone. Jupiter, through love, wants to make life easier and more successful. 444 is a triple threat of love, abundance and blessings!

Practise acceptance – of self, the situation and others. Allow your heart to blossom. 444 is the number of an open door to a sanctuary. Keep it open.

If you have been going through difficult times, this is a fantastic sign. 444 is a relief from hardship, conflicts and burdens. This is a truce. Take the kinder and gentler path. This can also be your reminder to be more accepting of the situation at hand.

Ease up – 444 is asking you to stop micromanaging everything. Instead, have faith in divine beneficence. Everything is working out for the highest good, and you have everything you need.

This is your message to be more open-minded and look at the big picture. Assess the situation fairly, examining the assets and liabilities without taking them personally. 444 is objective awareness. Trust that everything is trying to work itself out for the better and be open to all possibilities. You have everything you need in this moment.

Let go of the fear of failure and success. If you could do anything and not fail, what would it be? Perhaps there is a new opportunity, and you're nervous to make the leap. Make it. Lead with your heart, lead with love. Love dissolves fear. This is your sign that Spirit has your back. 444 is being protected by God.

Take a moment to simply be. Accept exactly where you're at. Relinquish regrets of the past and anxiety about the future.

Allow for honesty with yourself and others. This is a good message for mediation and conflict resolution. 444 is a truce. It is a safe space in which to share your ideas and feelings without fear of judgement, as well as an opportunity for you to be less critical and judgemental. After all, it is considered the number of sanctuary. If you are having relationship issues, this is your message to start resolving them. Love abounds. It is time to let go of anger and resentment. Again, this is a message of love, perfect love. It asks you to receive love and to be more loving. To forgive and be forgiven. 444 is redemption. Broken hearts can be put back together. Love heals all wounds.

This is also a fortunate sign for contracts, agreements, legal issues and working well with others. 444 is, in fact, the number that inspired me to write this book. Not because I was seeing it (honestly, I wish I saw this one more) but because a friend sent me a clip of a former US Navy SEAL speaking about numerology on a conservative-leaning podcast. It's an unusual place to hear numerology discussed, which is why my friend sent it. This military man was sharing that when he started dating his wife, he kept seeing 444 all over the place. He took it as a sign that she was the one. He admitted he had no idea what it meant, but it felt right. He said he searched for it online, and all he got was a lot of gibberish. I found myself talking to the screen, saying, 'Dude, 444 is the number of perfect love; of course you should have married her.' It was then and there that I decided I needed to write this book.

This is a nice number of easy blessings, obvious blessings. Not those in disguise. You know those: the trials and tribulations you have to endure, to learn from your mistakes until it finally works itself out, and you say, 'Actually, it turned out to be a blessing.' These are no-strings-attached blessings. If anything, the challenge is to trust.

**444 IS REDEMPTION.
BROKEN HEARTS CAN BE PUT
BACK TOGETHER (OR MENDED).
LOVE HEALS ALL WOUNDS.**

BE MINDFUL

Since 444 is a message of kindness, mercy and acceptance, it can also signify that you are being complacent and ineffectual. It can be a cue to avoid laziness and apathy. If you feel this might be your interpretation, it means it is time to start creating goals and taking action to achieve them.

PROSPERITY PRACTICE

444 is a message of good deeds and charity. Do good for others. Be generous. 444 is a gift that keeps on giving. There is a prosperity practice I love, which is to give a gift every day for 40 days. If you keep seeing 444, it might be a sign to start gifting.

444

IS:

PERFECT LOVE

BETTER THAN EXPECTED

TRUST THE MIRACLE

DOORS OPENING

EASY BLESSINGS

555

The Universe is giving you power. Use it well. What do you need to attack? Be ambitious. You can get what you want, but you might have to fight for it. 555 is a message to clear obstacles – or a sign that obstacles are being cleared for you.

5 is the sword. Now you have three of them. What is in the way of your goals? This is the sword used to cut away the obstacles, like a sculptor's chisel. The statue already exists. You only need to chip away that which is not the statue. You could also say that 5 is a scouring brush used to clean a dirty casserole dish, or an exfoliating facial scrub clearing dead skin and grime, giving you a renewed glow.

This is an awakening. The force of the Universe is giving you a revelation. Perhaps it's a wake-up call.

BE A TRAILBLAZER AND A PIONEER. 555 IS A DISRUPTER.

What needs to change? This is your moment. It's an awakening of clarity for your next life move.

555 is a cosmic alarm clock. It is time to wake up, get out of bed and go for it. This is a message to be more decisive – no more wishy-washy! As one of my teachers always said, this is not the time for fence-sitting. Stop idling, put the car in gear and step on the gas. The race is on. The good news is that 555 is a high-performance racing car.

In Qabalah, the fifth Sephirah is known as *Geburah*, which means 'severity' or 'power'. It is attributed to the planet Mars and the colour red. Mars teaches us how to take the right action. It is inspiring, invigorating and powerful. Mars is a go-getter, a self-starter and a pioneer and the Roman god of war. Mars is courageous and ambitious. Mars is also the self. What do you want for yourself? 555 is all of this intensified. The message is you have an army of energy supporting whatever you do. This is your cue to go for it. You might have to battle it out, but victory will be yours.

Whether with a sword or a pen, 555 is an editor. Again, what can be removed? What needs to be adjusted or modified? If you see 555, you are in the editing phase of a project. Ask yourself what needs to be edited in your life. If you feel as if you are a rough draft of yourself, that's okay. Here is your chance to clean up your act.

Be a trailblazer and a pioneer. 555 is a disrupter. Create something that will disrupt the status quo for the better. This can be as big as an industry-changing invention or, in my case, putting up shelves in the pantry, clearing the way for a new paradigm of organisation and tidiness. Victory was mine.

This is an excellent sign for a start-up business or something ground-breaking and innovative, such as an ambitious art piece or a home improvement project. Often, obstacles arise because you are going places no one else has been. Stay determined. Don't give up on your dreams. 555 is a risk taker.

It's time to get rid of dead weight. What is keeping you down? It could be relationships that no longer serve you or that pile of junk in the garage you've been planning to get rid of for years. Clear out the clutter. 555 is also about cutting corners. Not in a cheap way; this is about being efficient. A lean, mean fighting machine, as the saying goes. Where are you spending too much on useless outgoings, in business and personally? It's time to tighten your belt. 555 is a very focused force of nature. Don't dissipate its potential by being scattered.

When my wife and I were buying a new home, we finally found 'the one.' Leading up to viewing the house, and before we put an offer on it, I was seeing 555 constantly. I kept waking up at 5:55 on the dot (like I said, nature's alarm clock) and seeing number plates, addresses, receipts and even graffiti. Even my wife was noticing it. I knew this was a message about how to get the house. There were a ton of offers on the home we wanted, plus we had a newborn and a hard deadline to leave our rental property. I had to get the house for my family. It was a fight. I had to come in swinging with an ambitious offer.

In my offer, I put an escalation at intervals of 5,000. This means that if someone offers the same amount, my offer increased by another 5,000. I aligned with the fives I was seeing. Remember, 555 is also about what can be cut away. I forfeited doing a home inspection and appraisal. It was a risk, but if there's a number that takes a risk, it's 555. Well, we won the battle. Not only did we get the house, but the escalation never kicked in, saving us 5,000, and the appraisal and inspection turned out fine. I paid attention to the signs, and I knew how to proceed. We were destined to get the house, but the Universe told us how.

DON'T GIVE UP ON YOUR DREAMS. 555 IS A RISK TAKER.

BE MINDFUL

555 can be a message to tone things down. Calmer heads will prevail. Don't overdo it or try to force that which does not fit. It is a relatively volatile force. It might be a message to examine how you're overdoing it. Don't misuse the fighting energy of 555 as an excuse to create conflict, harm others or start arguing with everyone you encounter. It is a number of intensity. As with cayenne pepper, a little goes a long way. The teaching is to respond, not to react.

555 can evoke many fears, especially fear of loss or not having your expectations met. A key lesson here is managing those expectations.

PROSPERITY PRACTICE

555 is the energy of clearing what isn't needed. It is a liberator. Lighten your load. There is a prosperity practice: Let Go To Grow. Get rid of at least one item a day for 40 days. If you keep seeing 555, it might be time to clear the clutter. This will create space for new opportunities.

555

IS:

FORTUNE FAVOURS THE BOLD

THE BALL IS IN YOUR COURT

TRAILBLAZER

GLOVES OFF

THE ONLY CONSTANT IS CHANGE

666

You are being ordained with greatness. The number 666 is reminding you of your power. You have a higher purpose. This is your destiny. Spirit has a greater plan for you: you are being exalted. 666 is blessing you with confidence. You are capable, dynamic and talented. You are on the verge of making a big leap. You've got this; the Universe believes in you; believe in yourself. 666 represents your most enlightened self. You are being blessed with spiritual wealth. You are launching into a higher orbit. The number 666 symbolises harmonious expansion. Allow yourself to be the vehicle of Spirit. Go for it.

666 calls on you to be the best version of yourself and demands that you become a conduit of your higher self. You are merely a reflection of this divine power. Interconnect with it. Transmit this spiritual energy

in all your endeavours. Be radiant, but remember: God is the source of your radiance and power.

The number 6 represents higher connections and harmony. It is known as a person of prayer, one who is reverent and embodies divinity. In Qabalah, the sixth Sephirah is called *Tiphareth*, which means 'beauty'. This beauty is the glorious harmony of the cosmos. The sun (which symbolises your higher self) and the colour yellow are associated with it. It is important to remember that your best self is only a reflection of your divine self.

666 is one of the most misunderstood numbers. Often associated with the devil, it is, in fact, the number of humankind. It represents enlightened humanity. 666 symbolises the human race at its best, embodying ingenuity, capability and harmony, united by providence and working together in service for the higher good of the entire planet.

666 is signalling to you to create harmony and order. Start within and allow its orbit to expand from yourself to your home, family, community, and so on. This ripple effect will eventually expand to the far

reaches of the cosmos, uniting the microcosm with the macrocosm. 'As above, so below' is the spiritual precept in action here. Do the inner work, and it will affect your external world.

666 is a call for ritual and sacred acts. It symbolises exoteric spiritual practices (those one does in public), which are the reflexive of inner work. This is what you do externally, such as attending a religious or spiritual service, meditation, going out in nature and becoming one with it. Those are just a few examples. What you do for a sacred ritual is entirely up to you. If you don't have a practice, this is your message to develop one. 666 is consistency. The orbit of the Solar System is consistent. Your job is to reflect this. Develop a routine. Spirit is asking you to create a sacred and orderly space.

666 IS REMINDING YOU OF YOUR POWER. YOU HAVE A HIGHER PURPOSE. THIS IS YOUR DESTINY.

BE MINDFUL

666 is an awakening of your spiritual powers and facilities great ability. You can move mountains and achieve the goals you never thought possible. And therein lies the Devil. You didn't think we'd get off that easily, did you?

Understand that you are merely the conduit of divine energies and powers. This is why 666 is a reminder to keep connected to your higher self and to maintain a sacred practice. When this is lost, 666 becomes egomaniacal materialistic drive. 666 is a message to embrace confidence, but not delusions of grandeur.

When you dismiss your connection to a divine source, you become a materialist, thinking all you have in life is yourself and the physical world you live in. 'As above, so below' degrades to become low and lower. In the Hermetic tradition, Satan is that which disconnects you from the divine. Ultimately, this is a very dark and hopeless place to be. The wise understand that 666 is material wealth, while recognising that true wealth is spiritual wealth – which in turn will provide the material possessions you need.

The other devil is the demonisation of your own growth. 666 appears because you are afraid of your own success and power. Overcome your fear of greatness and remember that you have a higher purpose. A prayer taught to me, and one I say often, is, 'I agree to be great; I surrender to the greatness of God.'

This is a message to get out of your comfort zone. This is where dreams go to die. Your mind, or rather the Devil playing tricks on you, will come up with endless reasons why you shouldn't risk creating greater success and opportunity – trapping you in your comfort zone.

'I'm too old, I don't have the right credentials, I don't have the money.' Reflect on the barriers you create for yourself. Have you ever said, 'I will finally get my life together once I do this?' Or 'once I lose 25 pounds, I can start dating; once I move to a cabin in the woods, I will write that novel; once I quit smoking, I'll go to the gym.' Blah, blah, blah. Enough with the excuses and elaborate schemes that delay victory.

PROSPERITY PRACTICE

Do something that pushes you out of your comfort zone. For example, if you're anxious about public speaking, consider taking a public speaking workshop or improvisation class. Alternatively, muster the courage to apply for a promotion or request a pay rise. Learn a new skill. One practice is taking cold showers or cold plunges. It seems horrible at first, but most people report feeling invigorated afterwards. The idea is to push yourself.

666

IS:

DIVINE POWERS

GREATNESS

HUMILITY

CONFIDENT AND CAPABLE

ORGANISED

DILIGENT

HARMONY

CONSISTENCY

DESTINY KNOCKING

HIGHER CALLING

777

With a twinkle in its eye, the Universe is blessing you. 777 symbolises prosperity. It is a message of elevation: new heights will be reached. Improvements are underway. Things are looking up, and life is getting better – perhaps even luxurious. You're being upgraded from economy to first class. Enjoy this. This is excellent for enhancing your current situation, promoting self-improvement and encouraging others to improve. Be your best self. Take full advantage of this opportunity while also creating space for others to excel. 777 beautifies everything, making you look good and feel good. Conversely, when you feel good, you also look good. This is a cosmic makeover. What aspects of your life could use a refresh? A new look? A haircut, new clothes? Your surroundings? It could be a call to enhance your home, office or even your attitude. Whatever the case may be, this is your opportunity for improvement.

The number 7 is known as the platform of elevation – a place where significant leaps occur. It embodies a desire to improve and uplift. In Qabalah, the seventh Sephirah is Netzach, which means 'victory'. This Sephirah is associated with the planet Venus and the colour green. Venus symbolises love, art, beauty, creativity and intuition. She teaches us sensitivity, kindness and the appreciation of life's finer things. 7 represents prosperity and victory and 777 even more so. It's the icing on the cake. 777 is the jackpot.

When my wife and I moved to Vermont in north-eastern USA, I started seeing the number 777 everywhere, and I still do. Our post office box number is 777. We live near a sign that marks the highest elevation of Route 7, which is 777 feet high and close to Route 7A. Vermont was founded as an independent republic in 1777. It's called the Green Mountain State, and green is the colour associated with the number 7. You get the idea; a lot of 777 is happening in Vermont. This is where my wife and I elevated our lives. We bought our first house and became parents.

We get to work from home with beautiful mountain views and are members of a wonderful community.

This is a message to be more creative. It can be as literal as making art, but often it means taking a more creative approach. There is a more innovative solution to whatever problem you are facing. Be more intuitive than analytical.

777 is a message for gaining a deeper understanding of value. What do you truly love in your soul? 777 encourages you to align with what truly matters to you. While it represents a luxurious upgrade, recognise that true luxury is a deeper experience of your soul. The real luxury brand is you.

777 serves as a reminder to recognise your self-worth. When you appreciate yourself more, you become more valuable. Develop a practice of declaring your own worth, and this will help define what you are worth in this world. Acknowledge your talents as valuable resources. Release self-doubt and insecurity. It's time to pursue that promotion, although this doesn't have to be about your career. 777 is a sign that Spirit wants you to have the best life ever.

BE MINDFUL

As much as 777 signifies prosperity and luxury upgrades, it is wise to remember that all that glitters is not gold. 777 can serve as a warning about the illusion of success. Or getting ripped off. If it seems too good to be true, it most likely is. Are you being seduced into something that isn't right for you? Beware of the siren call that could lead you astray. Without self-worth and a sense of what is truly valuable to you, it's easy to slip into decadence and debauchery – constantly consuming something from the outside, attempting to fill a void that can only be filled with self-worth.

BEWARE OF THE SIREN CALL THAT COULD LEAD YOU ASTRAY.

PROSPERITY PRACTICE

777 is a luxurious upgrade. Seeing it could signify the opportunity to experience opulence. There is a prosperity practice referred to as The Opulence Practice. Indulge in something you wouldn't typically consider splurging on; let it be something you love. It can be as large as a new luxury car or as small as a bottle of exquisite olive oil. Do this within your means. I do not want to get a message from you saying I saw 777, so I leased a Bentley even though I can't afford it! Remember, 777 teaches us about true value.

777

IS:

ELEVATING

BEAUTIFUL

SENSUAL

EARTHLY DELIGHT

THE JACKPOT

ICING ON THE CAKE

LOOKING GOOD, FEELING GOOD

SELF-IMPROVEMENT

LUCKY CHARMS

OPULENCE

ALL THAT GLITTERS IS NOT GOLD

ROSE-TINTED GLASSES

888

The Universe is giving you a boost. This is an uplifting message. With it comes enthusiasm and a pep in your step. It's like a breath of fresh air. You will be provided for: 888 is blessing you with life-force energy. You are being recharged and revitalised. 888 is a message to aim high. You are being supported. Take it to the next level. This is the fuel needed for lift-off.

888 is longevity. It is a gift of endurance. What you do will have a lasting impact. Create something that will withstand the test of time. This is an excellent number for business and money. 888 is the number of good health. For a business, this means getting an infusion of cash, if you will. Scale up. This is a message of growth and expansion. On a personal level, this is a cue to improve your health and well-being. Start focusing on what you need for optimal performance. Whatever you are working on, it's going to grow.

The number 8 represents life-force energy. Prana, chi or life force – whatever you call it – powers your battery and boosts your confidence. It is considered the number of healers. In Qabalah, the eighth Sephirah is known as *Hod*, meaning 'glory'. The planet Mercury and the colour orange are attributed here. Mercury symbolises precision, accuracy and adaptability.

If you have been befuddled by a problem or your next move, 888 is showing up to give you clarity and confidence. The number 888 signifies blessings of power and brilliance. Work smarter, not harder.

888 is a blessing of healing and improvement. It's a message of restoration. Decide what needs improving in your life. 888 is here to help. It could be as simple as taking your vitamins or changing the oil in your car or as big as running a marathon or deciding to go back to college. The energy is there. It is up to you to direct it.

The universal life force is bequeathing itself to you, which also serves as a message to bring your dreams to life and achieve your goals. 888 is great for awakening lost dreams and revitalising old ideas and projects. It inspires you and reminds you that you can do this. It is the confidence boost you need.

The flip side of 888 is neglect and decay. Take a look at what is being neglected in your life. Have you ever neglected a houseplant until it is in a near-death wilt? I have. An embarrassing number of plants have needlessly suffered at my indolent hands. 888 is giving that poor plant water and sunlight. Before long, the plant will be alive and well.

I once fostered a dog. She was an adorable little white stray. When we first met, she smelled horrible, had awful breath and matted hair and was quite lethargic. I was determined to bring her back to her old self and find her a good home. She fully came alive after a few weeks of love, a great diet and professional grooming. No more smell or bad breath, either. During this time, I kept seeing a car with a personalised number plate, 888HAR, everywhere in my neighbourhood. I even encountered it while driving far from home. This was in Los Angeles, a vast city. I kept hoping it was a sign of money or perhaps I was supposed to know the person driving it. It finally dawned on me that 888 was confirming I was helping that dog, a little nod from Spirit. I am pleased to report that she was adopted by the nicest young couple who love her like crazy.

888 represents restorative powers. It is a beneficial number for recovering from illness or surgery, or even overcoming substance abuse and similar challenges. Remember, the number does not do the work for you. Use it as a reminder of what needs to be done.

All the life-force energy of 888 is like a natural fertiliser assisting in the growth of whatever garden you are planting, which can be a sign of fertility and perhaps pregnancy.

A traditional meaning of 888 is, 'The generations of the heavens and the Earth.' Maybe the family is growing. Perhaps it is a sign to connect with your ancestors or ancestral lands. What are you creating that will last for generations? It can be inheritance or generational wealth. It can also clear family curses, trauma and karma. Somebody has to do it: 888 might be the sign that it's you.

888 is eternity. The number 8 even looks like an upright infinity symbol. Again, think longevity. This is a message of sustainability: energy, environment, sustainable agriculture, perpetual motion and building for the generations that will come after you.

Nothing is written in stone except 888. A great bookshop in our town has a stone at the entrance with 'Nothing is written in stone' engraved on it. I always see it as 888 and think to myself, I hope they keep selling my books forever. One traditional meaning of 888 is to engrave. Again, create something that will last. Make it amazing. Be very mindful not to create something that may become malignant. If you see 888, it's a message that everything you are doing will set you up for long-term results, whether positive or negative. Ensure you are creating a healthy and constructive trajectory.

888 is closely connected to financial growth. Money is a form of life force; it is the fuel that sustains nearly every material possession you have. 888 conveys a message to enhance your wealth. If you are in debt, Spirit reminds you to become whole. 888 is a message of solvency.

BE MINDFUL

888 is a charged battery that provides all the energy you need. It is powerful and impactful, eager to keep going. It is wise to assess where you may be overdoing it. If you're spreading yourself too thin, you could crash and burn. Examine where your energy is leaking – time, money or health. 888 could be a message to rest and recuperate.

PROSPERITY PRACTICE

888 represents the pranic force (*prana* means 'life force' in Yogic philosophy). It is believed that the breath is one of the keys to unlocking its magic. Observing the breath can serve as a simple reminder to breathe. Move around to get the oxygen flowing. Step outside to enjoy some fresh air. There are various types of conscious breathing exercises. A Yogic teaching suggests that all will be well if you practise 11 minutes of conscious breathing daily.

888

IS:

LIFE FORCE

SUSTAINABILITY

HEALER

LEGACY

EVERLASTING

GROWTH

LONG GAME

GOOD HEALTH

CUP OF COSMIC COFFEE

BIG MONEY

FERTILITY

999

This is the beginning of the end. Your efforts are about to pay off big, and your goals, visions and projects are on the verge of coming to fruition. This is what I call the 'just about to' phase. You are not yet in the clear, so stay diligent and gracefully apply the finishing touches. Everything is coming into focus, and perfection is near.

If you see 999, it is the grace of an invisible hand. You are being helped in ways you may not recognise. 999 is the number of subtlety. It is multidimensional. It is the unseen realms. It is a message coming from an invisible place.

The number 9 is associated with what is known as the subtle body, representing refinement, grace and elegance. It is considered the master of all systems.

999 IS THE PENULTIMATE STAGE BEFORE YOUR GOAL BECOMES A REALITY.

In Qabalah, it is the ninth Sephirah, known as *Yesod*, which means 'foundation'. It is also referred to as the filter. Everything you hope to manifest must pass through this filter, which is the final step before reaching your goal. The moon and the colour purple are attributed to this sephirah. The moon symbolises our inner self and subconscious – a realm often shrouded in mystery. It is your psychic inner voice. It often guides without speaking, able to sense the unseen.

Renowned film director David Lynch used numerology he saw on number plates. If he noticed a triple number and his initials (he was David Keith Lynch) in order on the same plate, he considered it the best sign. It was an even better sign if it was on a nice car. He told a story about how, while heading to a big meeting about the now legendary TV show *Twin Peaks*, he saw DKL999 on a Mercedes. He knew then and there that the meeting was going to go well.

I find it fascinating that it was 999 because it was a message saying, 'The show is about to happen.' He also passed away in early 2025, which adds up to 9. The number 9 is the number of mastery, and I consider him a master of his craft.

999 is the penultimate stage before your goal becomes a reality. You may have a business that is about to launch a new product. You created it and worked out all the kinks. Now, it's ready to hit the market. This stage is 999. The hard work of development is complete. Your efforts are about to bear fruit. Maybe you've given notice at one job and are seeing it through until you start your new position. Or perhaps your offer was accepted for a new house, and you're waiting to sign on the dotted line. This can be a delicate and intricate phase, involving paperwork, lawyers and mortgage brokers. I still don't fully understand how it all works. When we completed on our home, I felt like I was one mis-checked box away from jeopardising the entire process. In the end, we prevailed and received our new keys. It's like in the movies where a bomb is about to blow, and a complex web of coloured wires must be cut in the right order to defuse it. Fortunately,

there is always an expert who knows exactly which wire to cut. 999 is that expert. In order to finish the job, one must proceed sagaciously.

999 is delicate, refined and sophisticated. It is a gentle flower ready to bloom. You have done your part. You planted the seed, watered it and nurtured it. It has grown, and now you wait. An invisible hand will open the flower. 999 represents that invisible hand, a subtle force supporting your success. Patience pays; let the invisible hand of 999 work for you. 999 embodies Spirit assisting you in ways you might not see or understand. After all, as the eighteenth-century poet William Cowper said, 'God Moves in a Mysterious Way.' 999 is that mysterious way.

TRUST THE UNSEEN REALMS

BE MINDFUL

Sabotage often occurs in the final stages of delicate work. 999 asks you to be meticulous and nimble. One wrong move could ruin everything. I know a guy who couldn't go on his honeymoon because he completed his passport renewal form with a purple pen instead of the required blue ink. Thank goodness he wasn't defusing a bomb. 999 calls for acuity. Take a deep breath, hold your nerve and use a steady hand. If you do that, you will succeed.

PROSPERITY PRACTICE

Since 999 symbolises skill and mastery, a valuable practice for prosperity is to strive for excellence whenever you encounter this number. Whatever task you undertake, do it to the best of your ability, regardless of its significance.

999

IS:

GRACEFUL

SMOOTH OPERATOR

LIGHT ON YOUR FEET

INVISIBLE AID

EFFORTLESSNESS

NIMBLE LIKE A CAT

BEGINNING OF THE END

PSYCHIC

SIXTH SENSE
(OR SHOULD I SAY 999TH SENSE)

1111

Spirit is with you. Make a wish. You have unlimited possibilities at play. The infinite Universe is flowing in your favour. Your destination is being revealed. Point yourself there and set sail. This is a free ride to a higher opportunity. This is a message of synchronicity, which is a mechanism of destiny. If you are seeing 1111, everything is aligning as it should. Not only are you on track, but the opportunities might be more significant than you thought.

1111 feels as if the Universe is lightening the load for you. Scale up, aim high. Let others handle the job for you. Teamwork is the dream work. In this case, it's Team Infinite. There's no need to complicate your life by doing it all yourself. 1111 asks you to create something that the Universe can embrace. Allow the Universe to take it on as its own. This will yield dividends, both spiritual and material. There's a smooth flow here. Do the work, and the Universe will meet you halfway, maybe even closer. 1111 signals passive income, royalties and compound interest. Create that which will create for you. Focus on what's in front of you, and let 1111 manage the outcomes.

If there's one number that people love to notice, it's 1111. I've probably had a thousand text messages over many years that said 11:11 at 11:11. There are businesses named 1111, customised number plates and a whole lot of tattoos. The list goes on. A TV show on HBO even tried to delve into 1111. The show confused me so much that I couldn't get past two episodes. Clearly, 1111 was a trope, and nobody knew what it meant. In my world, everyone loves the number, but nobody knows its meaning – which is kind of what 1111 means. It is so big and expansive that it almost becomes meaningless. Infinite possibilities can mean anything and nothing at the same time.

11 is the number of the infinite. It is vast, expansive and powerful. I often think of 1111 as the infinite multiplied by infinity. 1111 is a more potent version of 11. It is considered the number of sound. Sound

is the vibration of the entire cosmos. One of the teachings of 11 is to 'vibrate the cosmos, and the cosmos shall clear the path'. Use your sound wisely; what you express will shape your reality. Everything is intensified. 1111 amplifies. Reflect on what needs to expand for you. This is your sign to align with higher goals and a broader vision.

In Mystical Qabalah, 11 is the place of knowledge. It is also attributed to the Sirius star system. Sirius teaches us that we are connected to infinite divine realms, within and without. Sirius serves as the messenger of your enlightened and perfected self. This is your truth beyond all limitations, ego and doubt. Engage with your infinite self; doing so will attract the higher destiny you are meant to fulfil. 1111 conveys that you are more connected, powerful and capable than you realise.

1111 CONVEYS THAT YOU ARE MORE CONNECTED, POWERFUL AND CAPABLE THAN YOU REALISE.

1111 ENCOURAGES YOU TO TAKE A LEAP AND BEGIN. TRUST THAT THE WINDS OF SPIRIT WILL MOVE YOU IN THE RIGHT DIRECTION.

BE MINDFUL

1111 is so vast and powerful that it can serve as a reminder to stay above water. Get out of your head; there is a whole Universe out there doing its thing. Your problems are smaller than you think. If you're feeling overwhelmed and uncertain about what comes next, 1111 can be a signal to make a decision and stick to it. You can adapt or change course later. Is your head in the clouds? This is your message to start turning your dreams into reality. Its vastness can make it feel like you're drifting into ambiguity. Get more specific about what you want. The challenge lies in making a choice. Knowing what's right for you can be difficult when faced with infinite possibilities. 1111 encourages you to take a leap and begin. Trust that the winds of Spirit will move you in the right direction.

PROSPERITY PRACTICE

1111 is sound. This spiritual concept represents the vibration present in all the frequencies of the entire Universe. 1111 signifies amplification. There is a teaching I love: fall in love with your own sound. A great practice for achieving this is to start saying positive affirmations. Speak what you want into existence, using the present tense. For example, 'I am in a loving romantic relationship' or 'I own a beautiful home in the countryside'. Whatever it is, say it with conviction. Your sound will be amplified. Fall in love with it.

1111

IS:

SAY IT, AND IT WILL APPEAR

MAKE A WISH

GOING BIGGER AND BIGGER

SET IT IN MOTION

CONFIRMATION

INFINITE FLOW

AUTOMATION

INFINITE POSSIBILITIES

WISH GRANTER

REAP WHAT YOU SOW

1–99

NUMBER 1

This is a message about co-creating with the Creator. 1 is your soul. 1 represents a new beginning. 1 is full of potential, but it is up to you to see this new journey through to the end. Get centred and stay on track. Keep creating. 1 is known as heart over head. Follow your yearning and instincts.

NUMBER 2

Connections are forming. 2 longs to belong. It involves lovers, family and community. 2 loves to be in love. 2 conveys a message of allowing and receiving. Keep an open mind. Be cautious about being too trusting. Apply discretion.

3

NUMBER 3

Make your dreams come true. The essence of 3 is in transforming your bright ideas and visions into concrete outcomes. It conveys a message to take action. 3 symbolises construction and manifestation. It reflects a positive mindset, optimism and intelligence. 3 follows a strategy. Be mindful of being overly analytical and avoid falling into a 'paralysis of analysis'.

NUMBER 4

Life is becoming easier now. 4 represents divine miracles and blessings. This is easy street, so give yourself a break. It conveys the message of acceptance and peace, reminding you to keep an open mind and not to judge. Practise compassion. Love your neighbour. Be careful of complacency and laziness.

NUMBER 5

5 is asking you to clear the obstacles. 5 teaches its lessons by force. It is a disruptive energy. 5 in its highest virtue is right action. It is cathartic and cleansing, and sometimes it stings. Sometimes, you just have to shake things up a bit – but be aware of rash decisions or being a hothead.

NUMBER 6

Get organised. 6 represents harmony and signifies your connection to your higher self. Listen for the divine message. 6 embodies diligence and consistency. Reflect on areas where there may be discord. It is signalling you to create a routine. Follow through and finish what you started.

NUMBER 7

Victory is in the making. You are being upgraded! 7 is the number of beauty and luxury. Perhaps it's time for a makeover, for yourself or your surroundings. 7 sends a message to make the world a better, brighter and more beautiful place than you found it. It is known as the number of elevations. However, be wary of illusory success.

8

NUMBER 8

You have the energy to go where you want and do what you want. 8 is the life-force energy of the Universe. You're receiving an energy boost – I call it spiritual caffeine. 8 is a message to keep on keeping on. It is also a blessing of healing and health. Be aware of overexertion and fatigue; 8 could be asking you to rest.

9

NUMBER 9

Your current success depends on a delicate touch. You're almost there; your dreams are preparing to land. Like an air traffic controller, guide them gently and accurately for a safe arrival. One wrong move could jeopardise everything.

9 is sophistication and subtlety. It is the invisible world. You possess deep awareness and sensitivity; some might even say psychic powers. You can perceive what is unseen. 9 is the master of all systems. Proceed with grace. Let go of princess-and-the-pea syndrome; in other words, don't blow things out of proportion.

10

NUMBER 10

You are being asked to put yourself out there. Let your voice be heard. It looks like you're the one who needs to take the lead. Abandon the cave you've been hiding in, once and for all. This is your message to be a force of nature – large and in charge. 10 is the number of nobility. Your insecurities are now a thing of the past. On the contrary, this could be a message to tone it down. Make sure you're not shining like an interrogation room light. Too much 10 is obnoxious.

11

NUMBER 11

Take it to the top. What you are working on is meant to go big. What you're creating needs to be offered to the Universe, allowing it to handle the results. God is your employer. Momentum is working in your favour. Something in your life is meant to expand. Go with this flow. Ride this wave. Stay above water and don't succumb to overwhelm. Let inertia work for you, not against you.

12

NUMBER 12

The love of God is supporting your endeavours. 12 confirms that a beneficent and miraculous force supports you. You are protected, so unfetter yourself from fear and dread. 12 also indicates that wishes do come true. There's a saying, 'Be careful what you with for; you might just get it.' You can reframe this; you will receive what you ask for, so perhaps aim a little higher.

13

NUMBER 13

It's all coming together for you now.
13 is the number of higher love – universal love. It is love through unity. This is your message to embrace love in everything.
A blissful life awaits you. 13 encourages you to ease up; peace is prevailing.
Isn't it interesting that the number of love is one of the most feared numbers?
What are you afraid of? Release it with love.

14

NUMBER 14

Significant changes are happening. If they feel painful at the moment, consider this your message to have faith. It's all for your greater good. The number 14 represents powerful transformations and sacrifices. The good news is that you're only letting go of what holds you back from a more fulfilling life. 14 also involves separating all the pieces and reassembling them in a better way. This is a new and improved version. It can also indicate cutting your losses and moving forward. Let it go or get dragged back.

15

NUMBER 15

To build something new, you must destroy the old. 15 represents volatility, a destructive force. It is a wrecking ball; use it wisely. The idea is to direct this energy to clear out what no longer serves you. This can be as small as your junk drawer or as big as tearing down a dilapidated building, making room for a beautiful new home. 15 can also be a message to take precautions. A storm is brewing; make sure you are prepared.

16

NUMBER 16

Your efforts are paying off. 16 is a message of exaltation. You will be elevated, akin to receiving a promotion and a pay rise. This is the result of having a deeper understanding of the situation at hand. If you don't have understanding, this is your message to develop it. When you do, success will open up. 16 can also be a message to focus on the here and now. Daydreaming avails you nothing at this point. Stay grounded, and good things will arrive.

17

NUMBER 17

Your goals are starting to crystallise. Spirit is seeking even more clarity from you. What are your hopes and dreams? Make them known. The number 17 is a sign that the Universe wants to fulfil those dreams. Clarity is prosperity. This is also your message to start enjoying life. The idea of 17 is that the Universe loves to experience joy through your joy. It's like compounded joy: the more you give, the more you get. Enjoy.

18

NUMBER 18

It's about time you started having more trust – trust in the Universe, trust in yourself and trust in others. Perhaps you have been wronged in the past. This is your message to move on. Rid yourself of envy, spite and vengeance. Remember, resentment is like drinking poison and expecting the other person to die. You are only harming yourself. A life well lived is the best revenge, so forgive and forget.

Perhaps you were the wrongdoer; if that's the case, this is your cue to atone. The number 18 can also serve as a warning that you are being deceived. Stay vigilant against scams and scammers.

19

NUMBER 19

Mother Earth is providing for you. Big blessings are to be had. 19 usually offers material prosperity, but stay open to all blessings. 19 is great for financial gains, property and other tangible assets.

If you have been feeling stuck or succumbing to a mindset of lack, this is your message to move away from that mentality and embrace gratitude. This is your reminder to appreciate what you have. By doing so, you will be blessed with new opportunities. Have faith that the Universe always provides what you need.

20

NUMBER 20

Good fortune and unexpected miracles are coming your way – 20 is a lucky message. You are also being blessed with wisdom. The key is your ability to recognise and receive this goodness. Keep things simple and get out of your own way. Don't take anything for granted.

21

NUMBER 21

Stay true to yourself. Be authentic, with yourself and others. Don't lose sight of what and who you are. Are you making choices in your life based on a higher truth or your lower desires and insecurities? This is also a message to have a heart to heart, whether with yourself or someone else. Honesty will make big strides.

22

NUMBER 22

Connections and bonds are forming. This is a positive sign for collaboration and working well with others. The number 22 represents agreement and flow. It is a message of goodwill and a sign of a vibrant community. If you've been feeling lonely, this is your sign to make new friends and invite those who might also be lonely into your circle. Practise charitable acts.

23

NUMBER 23

Ensure you are clear on what you want and go for it. You will get it. 23 is desire and force. It is volatile energy. Use it to clear a path forward. Beware of conflicts and arguments and manage your expectations. If something is not meant to be, let it go.

24

NUMBER 24

You are cherished, and love and kindness are all around you. It's as if the Universe has a crush on you! This can literally mean you have an admirer and are the apple of someone's eye. On a deeper level, 24 asks you to approach life as if you have a crush on it. This will open a delightful path forward. It is also sent as a reminder that if you've been feeling low, your spirits will be lifted.

25

NUMBER 25

There is something you are not seeing. This is a message of clarification and a chance for breakthroughs. 25 is a fierce and destructive number; use it with discretion. What is holding you back? Clear your way. Whether it's the snow on your driveway, your lingering brain fog or a mountain of unresolved issues, the message is clear: now is the time. It symbolises both breakups and shakeups.

NUMBER 26

Choose the middle path. If you're going off the rails, this is your signal to get back on track. 26 symbolises balance and harmony. Stay calm, cool and collected. Maintain your centre – not too tart, not too sweet, just right.

NUMBER 27

Sometimes, all we need is a good cry. 27 is the number of goodness that results from overcoming grief. It is the transformation of tears of sorrow into tears of joy. It also conveys the message that time heals all wounds. Remember, this isn't about grief; it is about the glory of deep joy.

28

NUMBER 28

This is a message to begin expressing your creativity. Often, it relates to artistic creativity, as it involves beauty and the expression of beauty. However, it is also a message to start creating something, whether it's taking up photography or planting the garden how you've always wanted. Additionally, it is an excellent time for manifesting your goals. The number 28 is considered the number of creative force. Get creative with it!

29

NUMBER 29

Trim the fat. Sacrifices must be made. This number means to trim. It might mean literal weight loss, but it's also time to clean up your act. Where are you squandering time, energy or resources? It's time to look at the big picture and tackle what isn't benefitting you or the current situation. One meaning of 29 is to break into pieces. Analyse the situation granularly and remove the dross. 29 can also signify the end of a situation, but you must learn the final lessons to move on to greater opportunities. Wonderful things are on the horizon. You need to let go of what is holding you back.

30

NUMBER 30

Sometimes, you have to face life on its own terms. It is what it is. Don't waste your energy getting upset. There's a lesson to be learned from your mistakes; often, that's our greatest teacher. Practise humility. It's not a big deal. Accept it and move on. The solution is to correct your course, ensuring everything is moving in the right direction.

31

NUMBER 31

31 is a number of blessings, wealth and love. It serves as a reminder not to worry; remember that worrying is praying for things you don't want. A divine force is assisting you. Ask, and you shall receive. Don't let this opportunity slip by due to complacency and laziness. Great blessings are on their way.

32

NUMBER 32

It can all happen in an instant. The number 32 is symbolised by a lightning flash. This message indicates that success is culminating for you at breakneck speed. This is fulfilment and the realisation of your goals. Cut to the chase: what do you want? Get out of your own way and, boom, now you have it.

NUMBER 33

The stars are aligning in your favour.
This is a message of blissful abundance.
33 is a wellspring about to be tapped.
Your pity party has come to an end.
Enough of the ruminating: this is the river
of life cleansing you and washing away
your sorrows. Let go and let God in.
Go with this flow.

34

NUMBER 34

Now is a moment for forgiveness and humility. This is a message to be merciful to others. It might be time for you to move on, or it might be the occasion for admitting your own transgressions and absolving yourself. Either way, this is a message to examine what is holding you hostage. The price of freedom is forgiveness. It is time to get on with your life.

35

NUMBER 35

Full steam ahead. 35 is the power of God. There used to be a popular bumper sticker that read 'God is more powerful than a bomb'. This pretty much sums up one of 35's messages. It is also the number of spiritual and material treasures, and is considered the number of a ransom and means to redeem. In a way, this is saying you might have to pay a king's ransom, but it will be worth it in the end. In other words, go big! This is a message that your investment of time, energy and money will pay off. Commit and go all in.

36

NUMBER 36

The number 36 signifies a confession. The idea is to be honest with yourself. What are you in denial about? Get real, and opportunity will knock. 36 also represents agreements. This conveys a nice message about working through issues and that everything will turn out fine. There may not be disagreements, but if there are, it's a positive sign that things will smooth over. It is also an appeal to the Universe; 36 indicates that good terms will be agreed upon.

37

NUMBER 37

Think quick, be light on your feet and move nimbly. You might need to pivot and pivot fast. Blessings are trying to fall into your lap, but you need to be in the right place at the right time to receive them. Take a deep breath, clear your mind and become centred. In this headspace, it will be easier to make the necessary move.

38

NUMBER 38

The heart wants what the heart wants. 38 is a message to be vulnerable and follow your bliss. It's time to reveal your truth to the world. Be honest; spill your beans. This is your message to let go of shame and guilt. Your truth will set you free. Stop repressing yourself. You are who you are, and you're awesome. The message is that this will work out better than expected for you.

39

NUMBER 39

There is a hidden treasure you need to uncover. Remember, one man's trash is another's treasure. Be resourceful. See the beauty and value in everything. If you don't see God in all, you don't see God at all. It can also be helpful to step back and look at the bigger picture. What are you missing, or what are you taking for granted?

40

NUMBER 40

You are being blessed with a fecund garden. Keep tending it, and an abundant harvest will be waiting for you. 40 is the number of the waters of life, the womb and the mother. This is the gestation period. Stay at it, one step at a time. This is also a message to share your creative work with the world. You have a unique and special purpose. Begin showcasing your talents more.

41

NUMBER 41

You need to establish clear boundaries. 41 signifies strength and power. Get your act together. Where are you being too loose and casual? Now is the time for discipline. A boundary can also serve as a foundation. This message is meant to help you start defining the parameters of your goals by being more specific. Sharpen your pencils and get to work. You will have the ability to create something out of nothing.

42

NUMBER 42

This can be a warning sign: safety first. Take all the necessary precautions. Make sure you are prepared to weather the storm. The theme here is preparation, not calamity. If a storm does hit, 42 reminds you that it will pass. And if you're prepared, it won't be a big deal.

42 is also a cease-and-desist message from the Universe. Something needs to end – perhaps a behaviour, a job or a relationship. This is for you to decide. Remember that insanity means repeatedly trying the same thing and expecting a different result. It's time to throw in the towel and develop a new action plan.

43

NUMBER 43

This is a number of rejoicing. Go big or go home! Celebrate yourself. The Universe is reminding you how awesome you are. 43 symbolises greatness; it embodies big energy and willpower. One attribute is that of a lion or lioness. Stay bold and confident. Be the king or queen that you truly are.

44

NUMBER 44

This is a reminder not to compromise who you are or your values. Stick to your guns and don't betray yourself. 44 is considered the number that unifies wisdom and understanding, and it is the number of blood, sweat and tears. In other words, it is a message to put your all into the situation, even if it is challenging. Success will be the result of these efforts. 44 is also the number of births. The pains of labour will pay off. Roll up your sleeves and get to work. Your efforts will succeed.

45

NUMBER 45

Be a team player. This message encourages you to connect with others. It's wonderful for building alliances, whether professionally, creatively or both. In this context, the group can be much more powerful than the individual. 45 may also serve as a reminder to seek help. The number 45 symbolises a supportive community and is considered a number of humanity. How are you being of greater service to your community and the world as a whole?

46

NUMBER 46

Separation makes the heart grow fonder. What do you long for? This is a message to rediscover what has been lost: your dreams, your hopes, your desires. Don't give up on these. You are being reminded that you are meant to have a joyful life, one filled with loving goodness. This is a hopeful message.

47

NUMBER 47

Let loose and have some fun. It's okay to be silly or even a little foolish at times. The Universe is suggesting that you be a little less serious and more open. 47 embodies a revealing and playful energy. Generally, it signifies a good time ahead. The message is to be happy, joyous and free. Lighten up and enjoy the ride that Spirit is offering you. It's also time to dream big. Even if it's just a pie in the sky, embrace the fun. You might just get a slice. Just be mindful of being recklessly foolish.

48

NUMBER 48

This energy is forceful. It might indicate that conflicts lie ahead, but you will prevail. Come in strong and take what you want. On the other hand, it could be a message to tone things down. This is not a message of vengeance; it's a message of power and strength. It urges you to be direct. There's no time to prevaricate. Take action with conviction. Shed doubts and fears. You should know exactly what you want and go after it.

49

NUMBER 49

This is a fresh start and a new beginning. Turn over a new leaf. Perhaps you need a new approach. 49 also serves as a message about having a child; this might represent the start of a new project or endeavour as well as offspring. The number 49 also represents innocence. Renew yourself with a sense of wonder, so you can witness the miracles that surround you.

50

NUMBER 50

This too shall pass. If you are facing challenges, this is a message that blessings await after enduring hardship. There is light at the end of the tunnel. Good things are on the horizon. You will soon align with a more favourable set of circumstances. Fifty is a message of relief. Remember, tough times don't last, but tough people do.

51

NUMBER 51

You might have some growing pains. This is a message to keep trying. Don't give up. What you might perceive as a failure is just an opportunity for growth. 51 tells you that you will have success, but it comes with challenges along the way. Learn from this, adapt and keep going.

52

NUMBER 52

You can create whatever you desire by applying more discipline, structure and consistency. 52 is seen as a symbol of the bright, fertile mother and the earth – meaning the soil. In other words, you are working in fertile ground. What are you planting? The Universe is conveying that you have tremendous potential. It's up to you to realise it. Additionally, it represents understanding and wisdom. It also carries a positive message for teaming up with others to achieve a goal.

53

NUMBER 53

You can obtain what you desire and what you require. The key here is to allow yourself to receive it. The message emphasises that the Universe generously provides you with everything needed for your highest good. Let go of trivial desires, and the blessings will begin to flow. 53 represents wealth and abundance.

NUMBER 54

The Universe is conspiring to work in your favour. Get out of the way and allow this higher good to do its thing. This is a message to flow and permit. Release your attachment to needing to 'know' everything. Abundance is appearing in ways you couldn't imagine. Keep your mind open to new possibilities.

55

NUMBER 55

Your visions are becoming manifest.
55 is considered the higher frequency
of the earthly realm of manifestation.
It indicates that you are very close, that
your dreams are becoming real, and
that your efforts are about to yield results.
55 is also regarded as the mystical
number representing the fruit of the
Tree of Life, suggesting a hidden impact.
Your tree is about to bear fruit,
and success is imminent.

56

NUMBER 56

The Universe is ready to serve you if you will just be you. 56 encourages you to be yourself in the most honest and free way possible. Stop deceiving yourself and others. This is a message urging you to live an ecstatic life. When you create and interact from this honest place, all doors will open for you. Share what you genuinely love with the world, and truly cherish what you share. If you begin by falling in love with the life you have, then you will have the life you love. This change will transform everything.

57

NUMBER 57

It's time to adjust your course. *57* is a message to redirect, and represents a learning curve. The good news is you've taken the leap. Learn from your mistakes. Adjustments need to be made. It's also a message to just start, even if you don't have it all figured out yet.

58

NUMBER 58

A new day is dawning. 58 is the Morning Star. It is a message that your struggles are coming to an end. 58 asks you to move forward with strength and courage. It is also a message of love, kindness and grace. This can be a wonderful reset. It is a great sign for new projects and journeys.

59

NUMBER 59

What do you truly desire? 59 is urging you to fulfil that desire. Your power lies in your ability to attract it to yourself. This is also a number of sexual attraction, a positive indication of romance and love. If you're single, this is a great sign for attracting that special someone. If you're in a relationship, this is your cue to spice things up. 59 is also a message to get out of your shell and do something exhilarating and daring.

60

NUMBER 60

60 is the trial-by-fire number; it serves as a proving ground. Now is the time to prove yourself. You need to do what must be done. Don't hesitate. This serves as a reminder to release your doubts, have conviction and not to back down. Your resolve may be tested. This is a message never to surrender.

60 also conveys the message that you should never compromise your values. It represents honour and power. What doesn't kill you makes you stronger – your strength and dedication will bring blessings.

61

NUMBER 61

Like magic, you can create something from nothing. Make something from scratch. Wave your wand and make it appear. This is the number of negative non-existence as a portal to existence. Yes, you read that correctly. 61 is also a number of mastery. Proceed with excellence; you might be surprised by the opportunities that arrive. You can create value where there was none, like the alchemist turning lead into gold. Also, be mindful not to create problems where there are none.

62

NUMBER 62

See it through to the end – finish what's in front of you before moving on to the next task. 62 symbolises healing and commitment. This is your message to go all in. By doing so, you will experience tremendous growth and improvement. You are being blessed with enthusiasm, which will give you the endurance needed to accomplish anything you desire.

63

NUMBER 63

Be thankful for what you have. Avoid falling into the scarcity mindset by fixating on what you lack. The truth is, you do have everything you need in this moment. You need both to practise gratitude and adjust your expectations. 63 is a message to recognise the glory of God in everything. Miracles are happening all around us; begin to pay attention to them. The path to victory is to do the work and trust God with the results.

64

NUMBER 64

Why not just do what you actually want to do?! Do something for yourself. It isn't selfish to do what you need to do for yourself. This number is connected to desires. Not fanciful wishes but a deep soul yearning. It is asking you to fulfil this drive. It is a message to do what you love.

NUMBER 65

This is your message to step up your game. You need to take control of the situation. Amateur hour is over: it's time to go pro. You can rise above it all – as the saying goes, the cream rises to the top. 65 is an exalted state. This is the high road – you at your best, showing the confidence and discipline to maintain it.

66

NUMBER 66

Reveal your hidden gems. Stop hiding in your fear cave. No more holding back, no more censoring yourself. Show yourself, and the Universe will respond accordingly. You have incredible talents that need to shine. It's time to share your gifts with the world.

This is also a sign to get something off your chest. What have you been holding onto that should be resolved? Speak up for yourself before the issue becomes a deep-seated resentment.

67

NUMBER 67

67 is a number that distinguishes truth from falsehood. The fantasy is over. This message says you need to look at the big picture and assess what needs to happen to achieve the next steps. To deal with life on life's terms. Put your managerial cap on and get going. There is a teaching, 'When the pressure is on, start.' There is more work to do. It is time to address whatever responsibilities you have been shirking. Stop procrastinating. You will feel much better as you cross more tasks off your list. This is probably popping up because you are trying to create something significant.

68

NUMBER 68

The only thing you truly know is that you know nothing. It's time to let go of everything you believe you know. Empty your cup so new knowledge can fill it. Let go and grow. This is a message to listen and learn. Stop trying to prove yourself: perhaps you don't know best. It's time to build something new on a foundation of wisdom.

69

NUMBER 69

Start where you're at; create with the resources you have. This is your message to take a leap and understand that you don't need to figure it all out beforehand. You will sort things out as you go. It's a reminder to think on your feet more. Stop overthinking it. There is no perfect plan. It is just an excuse that's rooted in your fear of doing what you want.

70

NUMBER 70

Don't reveal too much. Less is more; be reserved. This is a message to button your lip and avoid jinxing a situation by oversharing. Speaking too much weakens focus and dissipates the energy, so stay steady and finish the job. As the saying goes, don't count your chickens before they hatch. If this is a negotiation, play your hand very carefully. Let the other person put their cards on the table first. Share on a need-to-know basis. Also, consider what is not being revealed to you – secrets are being kept.

71

NUMBER 71

Understand that it's going to take time. 71 asks you to keep going, even when things seem overwhelming. The weight of the world is on your shoulders, but you are being blessed with endurance. You are a diamond, but remember that you're still in the rough. Do your best to hold your head up high. The good news is that there's a faint light at the end of the tunnel, and it's getting brighter every day.

72

NUMBER 72

You are stronger than you realise. 72 is a sign to awaken your dormant powers. You are destined for greater opportunities. This is your call to pursue them. You are more capable than you imagine. Think of this as your pep talk from Spirit. You've got this.

73

NUMBER 73

The best way to predict the future is to create it. Your thoughts can determine outcomes. 73 is the power of the mind. This is your message to gain a clearer vision of your goals and aspirations. Focus clearly and be more specific about what you want. Maintain a clear mind.

NUMBER 74

You need to finish what you started. You are in it for the long haul, and it is your job to lead the way. You are the boss of the situation: take charge and get going. You are being called to be more disciplined, and your greatness is being forged.

NUMBER 75

You are being redeemed. The time is now to overcome your past, whatever issues, problems or hang-ups you might have. 75 is blessing you with resolution. She is alleviating your pains and sorrows. Set yourself free. Know that you are not alone: 75 is a message of love and charity. You can also lend a helping hand to someone else in need.

76

NUMBER 76

It's time for you to take a break. 76 is a message of rest and peace. This could be your sign to go on a relaxing holiday or, at the very least, to spend some time on yourself. 76 represents a respite from a hectic world. You are encouraged to look inward more often. Perhaps try meditation and get better sleep. 76 aims to soothe your nerves.

77

NUMBER 77

This message is one of devotion and surrender to a higher love, a greater cause and a deeper purpose. It signifies a new path for you – one of spiritual fulfilment. It serves as a reminder that you have a higher calling, and the Universe is encouraging you to start serving it.

NUMBER 78

Now is the time to begin a labour of love. This will be incredibly fulfilling for you. The number 78 is a sign to engage more in what you love in life. Level up your talents. This will be a life upgrade. Enjoy the process. Remember, it's not always about the destination but rather the journey.

NUMBER 79

You are a pillar of strength. The message is to support others, get involved more with your community and be of service. Help those who can't always help themselves. You are a guiding light. Stay grounded. It is also a message to work earnestly. There is a level-headed, down-to-earth sincerity with 79.

80

NUMBER 80

Trust your instincts. This is lightning-fast movement. There's no time to think it through. A part of you knows the answer way before you do. Embrace that; it's breakthrough time. The illusions and confusion are coming to an end. Your obstacles will be obliterated. The number 80 also conveys a message to let go of your attachment to the outcomes you think you desire. Spirit knows what is best. The message from 80 is guiding you there, whether your ego wants it or not. This is for the highest good.

81

NUMBER 81

There is a higher plan, and you may not be following it. If you encounter a detour, view it as an opportunity to pivot in a new direction. The path forward doesn't always align with your plans, but that's perfectly alright. You are being guided in a new direction. The message here is to embrace it. Don't get upset or resist it.

82

NUMBER 82

Take some time to relax. If you're pushing yourself too hard, it's time to rest. 82 symbolises tranquillity, rest and pleasant scents. It's like an indulgent spa treatment from Spirit to rejuvenate your soul. Take a moment to smell the roses. Create harmony through peace. It is also the number of kindness. The Universe shows kindness to you; return that kindness to others and to yourself.

83

NUMBER 83

Love is in the air. You are being blessed with divine love. This is a wonderful message for romantic relationships. Stay open to meeting that special someone. If you are already in a romantic relationship, this is your message to go deeper with it. It also represents the love of life and living with purpose. The number 83 signals wonderful companionship. This is the kind of love that melts a frozen heart. Take a moment to examine what feels stagnant and frozen in your life. Let this warmth unfreeze you and go with the beautiful flow.

84

NUMBER 84

Level up your personal determination and endurance, because great personal transformation is in the works. Go in with all your heart. The message is to stay dedicated and see it through to the end. Be convinced of your higher calling. This is the hard part, so hold your head high and keep at it. You will be victorious.

85

NUMBER 85

Every journey begins with the first step, and 85 is that step. This is your message to start something new. It could be a journey to a destination you've always dreamed of reaching. Perhaps it's finally time to launch that business you've been contemplating for years or to write that book you've always wanted to write. There are countless possibilities ahead. This is your message to take action. The number 85 also relates to the spoken word, so speak your desires into existence. A great way to do this is to express your aspirations in the present tense, as it will help bring them to fruition more quickly.

86

NUMBER 86

It's all coming together for you now. The number 86 signifies alignment. The message is that dreams can come true. It represents a divine flow – a flow that leads to your aspirations materialising. It is the connection between God and the Earth. Prepare in the practical earthly realm, and Spirit will provide. Get to work. This is also the number of universal creative power. Start creating, and the Creator will assist your creations.

87

NUMBER 87

The number 87 indicates you are capable of greatness, so don't compromise your standards. Stay vigilant. Determination will take you far. This number also symbolises truth and honesty. Own up to your mistakes and shortcomings and use them as a valuable opportunity for growth. 87 also serves as a reminder to mature and approach life more seriously. Be a person of honour and virtue. Get real. Be honest with yourself and others.

NUMBER 88

Embrace your secret powers. This is your reminder that you are more capable than you realise. 88 is the number of concealed spiritual powers: it is time to shine. One of the literal meanings of 88 is to be hot and to glow. Like the Donna Summer song, you are indeed hot stuff!

89

NUMBER 89

Get out of your rut. You are stuck in the inertia of your comfort zone. Stop procrastinating – there is plenty to do. Start tackling your tasks, beginning with just one. Turn inertia into momentum and inspiration. Soon enough, items on your to-do list will fall like dominoes. At its core, this is a message of liberation, but you need to work for it. The way out is through it.

90

NUMBER 90

Go within, and you will never go without. This is your message to listen to your inner voice. 90 is an inside job. Inner work creates outer success. 90 is also a number associated with deep meditation. Meditate more and take time for yourself.

91

NUMBER 91

Manna from heaven. Manna is divine nourishment. Big blessings are being bestowed. This serves as a reminder that the Universe loves you. It also conveys a message to recognise that miracles abound wherever you look. Consider the whole picture, big and small. Cultivate greater awareness. 91 is considered the throne of heaven. Gain a bird's-eye view of the situation.

92

NUMBER 92

Don't get stuck – you need a change. Personal growth can be daunting at times, and the number 92 is urging you to confront your fears. In which areas of your life are you afraid to grow? You are bogged down without realising it. Some of the meanings of 92 include mud, terror and mire. It's also said that the wise understand love, while the ignorant fear it. What are you afraid of?

93

NUMBER 93

You have a higher calling. This is your purpose, your destiny and your love. Start shifting into a more meaningful life. 93 is the number of living according to your divine purpose. This is a powerful number and your message to go for it all. What do you truly yearn to do with your life? This is a get-real moment. You are being blessed to live the life you are meant to have.

94

NUMBER 94

Get your mojo back. 94 is the spark to reignite your flame that is slowly dimming. It's time to release the burdens, the dead weight that no longer serves you. Examine how you're deceiving yourself. Release it, and you will grow. Don't give up on your dreams. 94 is also the number associated with unicorns. You are truly a unique individual with a special purpose that only you can fulfil.

95

NUMBER 95

Shatter that glass ceiling. This is a message of power, strength and vigour, meant to push the limits of what you thought was possible. It is time to break free from limiting beliefs and anything that is keeping you trapped. Be an impactful disruptor. Be a paradigm shifter.

96

NUMBER 96

You have nothing to prove. Maintain a reverent and humble attitude. 96 is traditionally the secret council of the divine. Tune into that inner voice. Get your head down and work hard. Lay your head low and do the work that needs to be done. This is a time to keep things to yourself. When we overshare, we can diminish the potential. 96 is great if you are working on anything new. There will be a time and place to reveal it all to the world.

97

NUMBER 97

Be on the lookout for a sudden blessing. Opportunity must be seized. God's grace is working in your favour, but you must pay attention here. It is also a message to be prepared to utilise these opportunities. Your success depends on your previous preparations. Be ready to seize the moment. As the Roman philosopher Seneca said, 'Luck is what happens when preparation meets opportunity.'

98

NUMBER 98

Bounty is coming your way.
This is the number of gemstones and treasures. Let's not complicate this one.
Big blessings are in the works.

NUMBER 99

The tribulations are coming to an end. Your hard work and efforts are about to pay off in big ways. Spirit is working alongside you, helping and favouring you with blessings of ease and great success.

INDEX

ACKNOWLEDGEMENTS

Thank you to my wife, Jeana, for all your encouragement, support and attention to detail. I couldn't have done it without you.

To my son, Isaiah Saint-Ra, and my daughter, Eleanor Rose, you are little angels (most of the time).

A deep and humble gratitude to all my teachers, seen and unseen. Your wisdom and guidance wrote this book.

Special thanks to Eve and the wonderful team at Quadrille / Penguin Random House.

And G, who gives the gifts that keep on giving.

ABOUT THE AUTHOR

Remington Donovan is a master numerologist and mystic seer trained in the spiritual wisdom of the ancients. He was quite literally born into the traditions of mysticism, spirituality and meditation, which naturally evolved into his over thirty-five years of experience in numerology and mysticism.

Along with performing thousands of private readings, Remington teaches and speaks all over the world and leads The Mystical Arts Mystery School online. He takes great joy in the gift of seeing life's highest potential through numerology and in using that gift to guide and transform others.

Remington lives in the enchanted Shires of Vermont with his wife, Jeana, and two children, along with many crystals and trees. He unironically believes in the infinite possibilities of the Universe. He is the author of *Numerology: A Beginner's Guide to the Spiritual Meaning of Numbers* and *Prosperity Practices: Harnessing the Power of Positive Thinking to Get the Life You Want*.

Quadrille, Penguin Random House UK, One Embassy Gardens, 8 Viaduct Gardens, London SW11 7BW

Quadrille Publishing Limited is part of the Penguin Random House group of companies whose addresses can be found at: global.penguinrandomhouse.com

Penguin Random House UK

Published by Quadrille in 2025

www.penguin.co.uk

A CIP catalogue record for this book is available from the British Library

ISBN 9781837834167
10 9 8 7 6 5 4 3 2 1

Managing Director: Sarah Lavelle
Publishing Director: Kate Pollard
Senior Commissioning Editor: Eve Marleau
Managing Editor: Chelsea Edwards
Copy Editor: Clare Double
Proofreader: Caroline West
Indexer: Helen Snaith
Designer: Claire Warner Studio
Design Manager: Katherine Case
Senior Production Controller: Martina Georgieva

Colour reproduction by p2d

Printed in China by RR Donnelley Asia Printing Solution Limited

The authorised representative in the EEA is Penguin Random House Ireland, Morrison Chambers, 32 Nassau Street, Dublin D02 YH68.

FSC
www.fsc.org
MIX
Paper | Supporting responsible forestry
FSC® C018179

Penguin Random House is committed to a sustainable future for our business, our readers and our planet. This book is made from Forest Stewardship Council® certified paper.